FAR-OUT and UNUSUAL

pets

Hairless Cats
Cool Pets!

Alvin and Virginia Silverstein
and Laura Silverstein Nunn

Enslow Elementary

an imprint of

 Enslow Publishers, Inc.

40 Industrial Road
Box 398
Berkeley Heights, NJ 07922
USA

http://www.enslow.com

Enslow Elementary, an imprint of Enslow Publishers, Inc.

Enslow Elementary® is a registered trademark of Enslow Publishers, Inc.

Library of Congress Cataloging-in-Publication Data
Silverstein, Alvin.
 Hairless cats : cool pets! / by Alvin Silverstein, Virginia Silverstein, and Laura Silverstein Nunn.
      p. cm. — (Far-out and unusual pets)
 Includes bibliographical references and index.
 Summary: "Provides basic information about hairless cats and keeping them as pets"
—Provided by publisher.
 ISBN 978-0-7660-3688-8
 1. Sphynx cat—Juvenile literature. I. Silverstein, Virginia B. II. Nunn, Laura Silverstein. III. Title.
 SF449.S68S55 2012
 636.8—dc22
                                       2009043925

Printed in the United States of America

102011 Lake Book Manufacturing, Inc., Melrose Park, IL

10 9 8 7 6 5 4 3 2 1

Photo credits: Alex Rave, p. 39; ALEXANDER NATRUSKIN/Reuters /Landov, p. 38; Anna
Prokhorova , p. 27; Getty Images, p. 22; iStockphoto.com: © Anna Utekhina, p. 37, © Burak
Demir, p. 4 (right), © Jacqueline Hunkele, p. 23, © Vladimir Suponev, p. 31; © Jean Michel Labat/
Ardea, p. 35; © John Robertson/Alamy, p. 15; Shutterstock.com, pp. 1, 3, 4 (left), 6, 8, 10, 13,
19, 21, 25, 42, 43, 47; Sunny Ripert, p. 29; © WILDLIFE GmbH/Alamy, p. 16.

Illustration credits: © 2010 Gerald Kelley, www.geraldkelley.com

Cover photo: Shutterstock.com

Contents

A hairless cat (left) looks like an ordinary cat with its hair shaved off!

1

Bald and Beautiful

Cats are known for their soft, fluffy fur. But the hairless cat is a bit of an oddball in the cat family. It looks like someone shaved off all its fur! Actually, it was born that way. And it will live its whole life without any fur.

Many people keep hairless cats as pets. They believe there is more to these cats than their unusual looks. In fact, hairless cat owners would say that to know them is to love them.

Even though a hairless cat looks like it doesn't have any fur, its body is actually covered with very short, thin hairs. You can see them if you look closely. They're easiest to see on the cat's ears,

Hairless cats may look like they don't have any hair at all, but if you look closely you can see short, thin hairs covering their bodies.

nose, tail, and paws. The hairless cat's body is smooth and silky. Stroking it feels like touching a fuzzy peach.

Hairless cats have become popular pets. Most of them belong to a breed called the Sphynx cat.

Got a Cat Allergy?

Achoo! Every time you go near a cat, you start sniffling and sneezing. You might think that owning a hairless cat would solve that pesky cat allergy problem. Actually, it is not the cat's hair that makes you sneeze or get itchy red eyes. Cat allergies are caused by dander—dead flakes of skin!

Although hairless cats do not have fur, they *do* have dander. So if you have a cat allergy, even a hairless cat may not be allergy-proof.

Big eyes and batlike ears make hairless cats very interesting to look at.

This is a rather new breed. In fact, Sphynx cats have been around only since the 1970s.

Sphynx cat owners love their pets' playful and loving personalities. Big, lemon-shaped eyes and large, batlike ears add to the cats' interesting looks. Read on to find out more about why hairless cats are truly far-out and unusual pets!

Far Out!

What's Hair Got To Do with It?

Most pet cats have fur. But some have a lot more fur than others. Long-haired cats can have hairs as much as 15 centimeters (6 inches) long. They need a lot of extra brushing and baths to keep their fur soft and silky. Persian and Maine Coon cats are popular long-haired breeds.

The fur of short-haired cats feels smooth, like satin. Siamese and Abyssinians are popular short-haired breeds.

In a world of furry cats, hairless cats really stand out. The Sphynx cat, the most popular hairless breed, has shown that fur has nothing to do with being a cool cat.

2

Where Did Hairless Cats Come From?

Hairless cats have been around since at least the 1300s. Mexican paintings from that time show pictures of them. Did today's hairless breeds come from those Mexican pets? Probably not. By the early 1900s, the Mexican breed had mostly died out. So where did today's hairless cats come from?

The First Modern Hairless Cat Breed

The hairless cats that we know today first appeared in Toronto, Canada, in 1966. A black and white

It's All in the Genes

How did hairless cats show up in a world of furry cats? It all comes down to genes. Genes are chemicals that are passed down from parents to their babies. In all living things, these chemicals control what features they will have, such as eye or hair color. Most cats carry genes for short or long hair. Hairless cats appeared because one or more of these genes somehow changed.

pet cat named Elizabeth gave birth to a hairless kitten in a litter of shorthairs. The owner named the hairless kitten Prune because of his wrinkly, naked body. Prune and his mother were bought by breeders, who wanted to use them in a new breeding program. When Prune was old enough, the breeders mated him to his mother and produced more hairless kittens. At first, this new breed was called the Canadian Hairless.

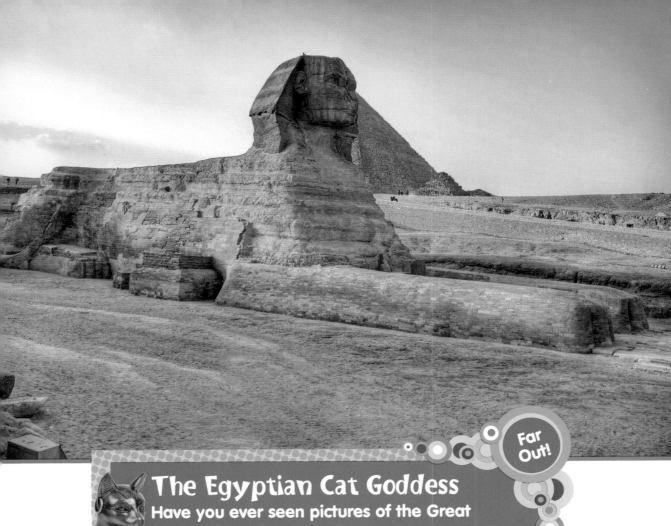

Far Out!

The Egyptian Cat Goddess

Have you ever seen pictures of the Great Sphinx of ancient Egypt? Sphynx cats don't really look anything like this famous statue (above). The Egyptian Sphinx has the heavy body of a lion and the head of a man. Sphynx cats look much more like the statues of the Egyptian cat goddess, Bastet. The Bastet statues look more catlike, with a lean body and large eyes and ears.

In the 1970s, the breed was renamed Sphynx, like the famous Egyptian statue. (The Egyptian statue is actually spelled Sphinx, though.)

Soon the hairless cats were recognized as a new breed by the Cat Fancier's Association (CFA). However, many of the kittens had health problems. The CFA announced in 1971 that Sphynx cats could no longer compete in cat shows because of their health problems. It looked as though the Sphynx breed might be doomed. Then in 1975, a cat named Jezabelle gave birth to a female hairless kitten, Epidermis.

The following year, Jezabelle produced Dermis, another hairless female. Kim Mueske, an Oregon breeder, used Epidermis and Dermis in a breeding program. She produced a new line of Sphynx cats.

Meanwhile, Shirley Smith, a Toronto cat breeder, rescued two homeless kittens in 1978. The kittens were brother and sister, but only the male was hairless. The female had long hair. But she later gave birth to two hairless female kittens,

The Sphynx breed started out as a popular breed at cat shows and then became a popular breed for pets.

Punkie and Paloma. These two females were the start of another line of Sphynx cats.

Breeders worked with the two new lines of hairless cats. By mating them with shorthaired cats, the breeders got rid of most of the health problems.

This cat is of the Don Sphynx breed, which originated in Russia.

In February 1998, the CFA finally accepted the Sphynx breed again. After hairless cats became popular as show cats, people soon discovered that they were fascinating pets. These cats were so unusual looking! They were lovable, too. Soon hairless cats became popular in people's households.

Other Hairless Cats

Hairless cats are still popping up from time to time in the litters of furry house cats and street cats. A new hairless breed appeared in 1989, in the Russian city of Rostov-on-Don. A hairless stray cat named Vanya and a local tomcat were the parents. The new hairless breed was named the Don Sphynx breed.

3

Caring for Hairless Cats

The old saying "Don't judge a book by its cover" could easily refer to hairless cats. Some people may think they look too strange without fur. But hairless cats are just as sweet and lovable as any furry cat pet.

Ready to Buy a Hairless Cat?

If you're looking for a hairless cat breed, you're looking for a Sphynx. So where can you buy one? Can you pick up a hairless cat from a pet store? Probably not. Hairless cats are usually sold by Sphynx breeders. You can find many of them by searching on the Internet.

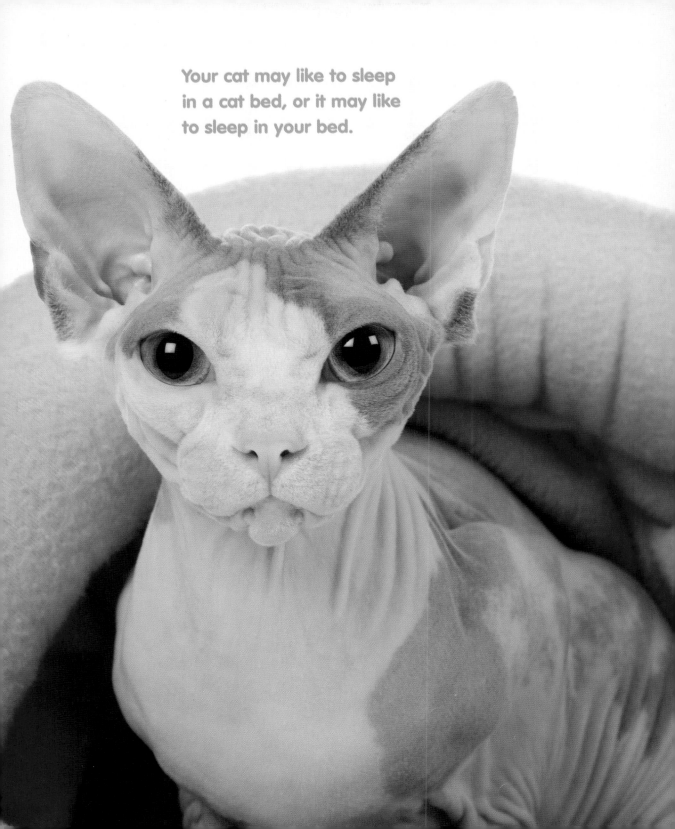

Your cat may like to sleep in a cat bed, or it may like to sleep in your bed.

What will you need for your new pet? Hairless cats eat the same kind of cat food as other house cats. You'll need two feeding bowls—one for food and another for water. Cat litter and a washable litter box are a must, too.

You can buy a cat bed at a pet shop or grocery store. But your pet Sphynx will probably be even happier sleeping on your bed. Make sure that its sleeping place is warm, though. Without a fur coat, your cat can get pretty cold! You may need to get some cat sweaters, too, for chilly days and nights. In general, if you need a sweater, so will your Sphynx.

A scratching post will help keep your cat from scratching your furniture. Cat toys can keep it from getting bored. Mouse-shaped stuffed toys and small balls to roll

You should give your cat toys to keep it from getting bored.

around are good choices. So are toys that tinkle, chirp, or squeak. Toys you can dangle on a string are fun for both you and your pet.

One thing you *don't* need is a cage. Cats like to roam around. They'll choose favorite places in the house to play and sleep.

Cats can use their gripping toes and claws to hang on to objects— or people!

A Mother's Love

Have you ever seen a mother cat pick her kitten up by the scruff of the neck? It looks almost like she's biting it! Actually, the mother cat grabs the kitten by the loose skin on the back of its neck and carries it to where she wants it. She's not hurting it at all.

Far Out!

The Sphynx Up Close

The Sphynx is a medium-sized cat with a strong, lean body. It has a long neck, large ears, and long, slender legs. It can use its long, gripping toes to pick up small objects. The fine hairs that cover its body are so small and light-colored that this cat looks hairless. A Sphynx may have short, curly whiskers or no whiskers at all.

The Sphynx's skin is wrinkled, but it doesn't really have more wrinkles than other cat breeds. All cats have rather loose skin, which falls into wrinkles when they are not stretching out. You can't see the wrinkles of other cat breeds because they are covered by the cat's furry coat.

The Sphynx comes in a variety of colors and patterns. Normally, colors appear on a cat's furry coat, but the Sphynx's colors show up on its skin, like a tattoo. Some of the colors may include white, black, orange, brown, and gray. They may appear in patches on the body.

Although Sphynx cats don't have any fur, they can still have different colors and markings, like spots or stripes.

There are also Sphynx cats with tabby-cat stripes, and even some like Siamese cats, with dark-colored face, ears, and paws.

A cat's normal body temperature is about 101°F (38°C), higher than the normal temperature for humans (98.6°F, 37°C). So its body feels warm to the touch. The thick hair on a furry cat acts like a blanket. It holds heat in, close to the cat's body. Without this warm blanket of fur, a hairless cat can get really chilled in cool weather.

Actually, Sphynx cats often prefer to stay indoors, especially when it is cold outside. In fact, hairless cats shouldn't go outside even on a warm, sunny day. Without fur, they can get a painful sunburn.

The Sphynx cat needs to eat more than other cat breeds. Without a fur coat, it loses body heat through its skin. So the Sphynx cat needs extra food to produce enough energy to keep its body warm.

Your hairless cat may get cold, so you may want to give it a sweater.

Do Hairless Cats Need Grooming?

A hairless cat means no grooming, right? Actually, no. Even though a Sphynx doesn't have much hair to clean, this cat is definitely not maintenance-free. A cat's skin produces oils, which normally soak into its fur. But a Sphynx doesn't have fur. So these oils gradually build up on its skin. The skin may feel sticky. House dirt will start to stick to it, making it look dirty. It may leave oily stains on your furniture. And if you don't

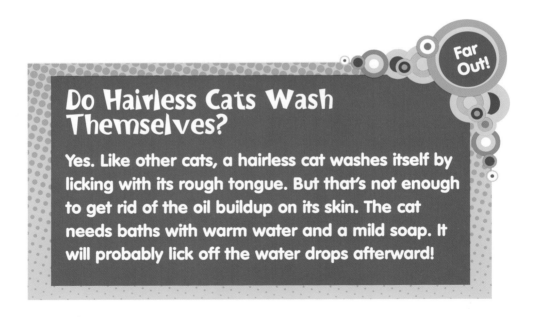

Do Hairless Cats Wash Themselves?

Far Out!

Yes. Like other cats, a hairless cat washes itself by licking with its rough tongue. But that's not enough to get rid of the oil buildup on its skin. The cat needs baths with warm water and a mild soap. It will probably lick off the water drops afterward!

Cats normally bathe themselves, but Sphynx cats need extra help. Oil builds up on their skin and can make them feel sticky if you don't bathe them regularly.

bathe your Sphynx regularly, it may have skin problems.

Cats usually don't like getting wet. But if they are bathed as kittens, they tend to be calmer about being washed as adults. To make it easier for the cat, you can use a washcloth rather than putting it in the tub.

A Lovable Personality

The Sphynx cat enjoys being around people. It also gets along quite well with other pets in the household. The Sphynx is very smart and curious and loves to investigate things of interest. It will follow you around the house, like a puppy, to see what you are doing.

The Sphynx is very adventurous and a little mischievous. This active cat may dash around the house and knock over things in its way. It may then give a look as if to say, "Who, me? What did I do?" It is a good idea to put away any breakables when there's a Sphynx in the house! Yet this bundle of energy enjoys a cozy nap in its owner's lap or some other warm spot. The top of a clothes dryer will do nicely. At night, the Sphynx will likely sneak under the covers of its owner's bed.

The Sphynx is a very smart breed. These cats can be trained to walk on a leash. Many have been

Sphynx cats like to play with toys, people, or other pets in the house.

taught to play fetch. They can also learn to use the toilet! You will need to spend a lot of time with your cat to teach it tricks. Using cat treats as a reward can help.

Is My Cat Crazy?

Your hairless cat may sometimes do things that puzzle you. Why does it want to play at night when you want to sleep? Why does it rub its cheeks against you? Why does it crouch down and creep along after a string that you drag along the floor? Why does it kill mice even though you feed it every day?

Sometimes it may seem like your cat is acting a little crazy. But cats only do what comes naturally to them. House cats—including hairless cats—behave very much like cats that live in the wild. In the next chapter, you'll learn about how wild cats live in nature. This can help you understand why your pet cat acts the way it does.

4

Wild at Heart

Hairless cats may not look like most other cats. But they are still *cats*. They have the same body shape as other house cats. They act like them, too.

When you take a hairless cat into your home, it can soon become a loving friend. You can have a lot of fun playing with it. But it will do some things that surprise you. Sometimes it may annoy you.

You can enjoy your pet cat more if you understand why it acts the way it does. Today's house cats—including the hairless ones—still do many things very much like their wild relatives.

The First Cat Pets

Cats were first tamed about ten to twelve thousand years ago! Scientists believe this happened in the Middle East, in what is now Israel and nearby Arab countries.

How did these wild cats become tame? It probably happened after people started growing and storing food crops. Rats and mice sneaked in and ate the stored food. Local cats caught and ate the rats and mice. Farmers were grateful for the cats' help in controlling these pests. After a while, people invited the cats into their homes. They gave them food and shelter, and found that cats made great companions.

Cats and Their Wild Ways

In the wild, cats hunt. They eat other animals. But a house cat has no need to hunt, does it? Its owner usually supplies it with plenty of food. And yet, house cats find it hard to resist chasing after a mouse.

All cats have an instinct for hunting.

Hairless cats are especially playful. They may run and jump, trying to catch an insect flying around the house. They may also toss small objects into the air and carry them around.

A cat has soft paw pads on the bottoms of its feet. They help it move quietly. Its long, curved claws don't make any noise when it walks on rocks or floors. That's because it can pull them up into its paws. But when the claws are out, they are great tools and weapons. The cat uses them to catch small animals, fight other cats, and climb trees. Cats' strong hind legs also make them good jumpers. If a cat falls, it twists and turns in midair. That's why cats nearly always land on their feet.

A Cat's Senses

A cat's senses are good for hunting. Cats' eyes are really good at seeing motion. They can quickly spot a scurrying mouse or a leaping grasshopper.

Have you heard that cats can see in the dark? That's mostly true. But they can't see in *complete*

knee

heel

Where Is a Cat's Knee?

Cats walk on their toes. Their legs (especially the hind legs) look like they're bending the wrong way because the part that bends backward actually is like our heels. Their knees are farther up on their legs.

Far Out!

darkness. A layer at the back of their eyes makes dim light brighter. So they can see fairly well in moonlight or starlight. This is a useful ability for wild cats, which hunt mostly at night. House cats may like to be active at night, too. So if you sleep with your hairless cat, it may wake you up and want to play.

Cats have much better eyesight than humans. A layer at the back of their eyes makes dim light brighter.

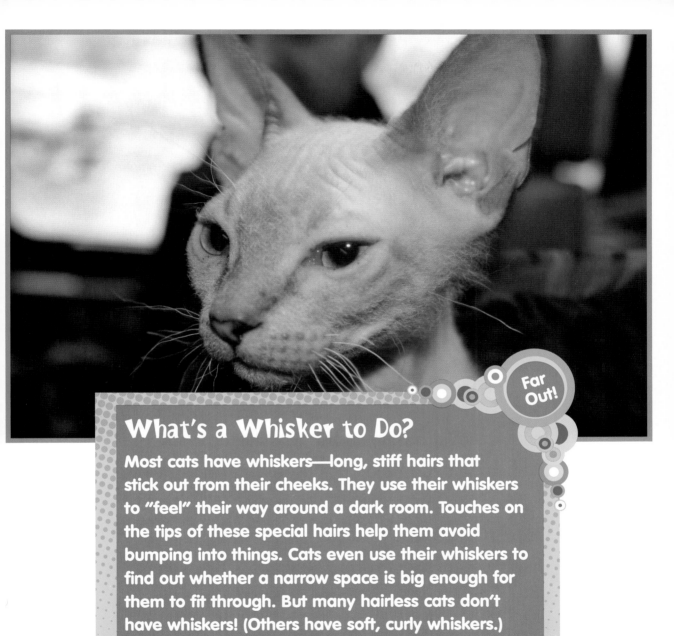

What's a Whisker to Do?

Most cats have whiskers—long, stiff hairs that stick out from their cheeks. They use their whiskers to "feel" their way around a dark room. Touches on the tips of these special hairs help them avoid bumping into things. Cats even use their whiskers to find out whether a narrow space is big enough for them to fit through. But many hairless cats don't have whiskers! (Others have soft, curly whiskers.) They get around just fine, though.

Cats don't depend on their eyes as much as we do. They use their senses of smell, hearing, and touch when they hunt. Cats have a much better sense of smell than people do. (If you feed your pet cat mixed dry food, you'll see it sniffing—not looking—around the bowl to find the tasty bits.) Cats can hear sounds too high-pitched for our ears. Mice and other small animals make these high-pitched sounds. A hunting cat also uses the sensitive pads on the bottom of its feet. It can feel the patter of mice running across the floor.

A Cat's Life

Except for lions, cats in the wild live a rather independent life. Each has its own territory, which includes hunting grounds and places to rest and sleep. (Cats spend a *lot* of time sleeping.) They mark their home territory by smell. They spray urine on bushes, trees, and rocks. Rubbing against things leaves more scent markers from chemicals made in their skin.

You Are Mine

When your pet cat rubs her cheek against you, she's not just showing her love. She's marking you. Her scent is like a sign saying, "This human belongs to me!"

Kittens in the wild are completely helpless at first. When they are born, their eyes and ears are still sealed shut. Their mother feeds them milk made in her own body. She licks them with her tongue to keep them clean. As the kittens grow, they learn to eat and wash themselves. They play and fight with the other kittens in the litter. Their mother teaches them important life skills, like hunting. When they are old enough to take care of

Kittens are small and helpless when they are born, but they learn important life skills as they grow.

Sphynx cats are friendly with their owners and with each other. They make wonderful pets.

themselves, the young cats go off to find their own territories.

Wild cats can be somewhat friendly, though. They may spend time lying around with other cats in the area. They like to lick each other's fur. Today's house cats generally have this kind of behavior. It has helped them become lovable pets.

Hairless cats have come a long way from their wild relatives. In fact, they probably could not survive in the wild. So keeping them as pets is a big responsibility. But with good care and a loving home, these far-out and unusual cats make wonderful pets. You can share fun and love with a hairless cat for fifteen years or more.

Words to Know

allergy—The body's overreaction to a normally harmless substance, resulting in a rash, sneezing, breathing problems, or other symptoms.

dander—Flakes of dead skin.

dermis—The layer of skin under the epidermis (the outer layer of the skin).

genes—Chemicals inside each cell that carry information for traits (such as hair color or hair length).

grooming—Cleaning an animal's fur or skin.

litter—A group of young animals born to the same mother at the same time.

territory—The area where an animal lives and gets its food. Some animals will defend their home territory against others of their own kind.

Learn More

Books

Furstinger, Nancy. *Sphynx Cats*. Edina, Minn.: ABDO Publishing Co., 2006.

Jones, Annie. *All About Cats*. Chelsea Publishing House, 2005.

Miller, Connie Colwell. *Sphynx Cats*. Mankato, Minn.: Capstone Press, 2009.

Ring, Susan. *Cat: My Pet*. New York: Weigl Publishers, 2009.

Web Sites

"The Cat Fanciers' Association, Inc."

<http://www.cfainc.org/breeds/profiles/
sphynx.html>

*This site gives the official Breed Profile of the Sphynx: its
appearance, typical behavior, and standards for show cats.*

"Purebred Cat Breed Rescue Org."

<http://purebredcats.org/sphynx.htm>

*This site provides contact information for organizations that
rescue unwanted pedigreed cats and place them in good
homes.*

"Fanciers Breeder Referral List"

<http://www.breedlist.com/sphynx-breeders.
html>

*This site provides contact information for Sphynx breeders.
It is organized by location: states in the United States and
countries in the rest of the world.*

Index